To:
From:

Sister 2 Sister

copyright © 2002 by Andrews McMeel Publishing. All rights reserved. Printed in Malaysia. No part of this book may be used or reproduced in any manner whatsoever without written permission except in the case of reprints in the context of reviews. For information, write Andrews McMeel Publishing, an Andrews McMeel Universal company, 4520 Main Street, Kansas City, Missouri 64111.

Illustrations copyright © 2002 by Ali Douglass
Text copyright © 2002 by Cate Holly

ISBN: 0-7407-1934-3

Library of Congress Catalog Card Number: 200187916

Sister2Sister

Written by Cate Holly
Illustrated by Ali Douglass

Andrews McMeel Publishing

Kansas City

"The best thing about having a sister was that I always had a friend."
—Cali Rae Turner

The only thing better than a sister

is a sister with the same shoe size.

My sister...
My first friend,
My best friend,
Till the end!

Smart
Interesting
Stylin'
Totally Tantalizing
Extraordinary
Radiant

Everyone should be lucky enough to have a sister.

"A sister is both your mirror...

and your opposite."
— Elizabeth Fishel

We branch out in different ways...

Lord help the mister
who comes between
me and my sister
And Lord help the sister
who comes between
me and my man!

—from the movie
  <u>White Christmas</u>
   (sung by Bing Crosby
    and Danny Kaye in drag!)

Sisters are a fail-proof,

One sister is v. cool...

Two sisters is incredibly awesome...

Three sisters is knowing you'll never get a bedroom to yourself!

Our little fights never last long... and always seem silly the next day.

Nothing comes between sisters . . .

unless he's really cute.